Inspiration & Wisdom from the Pen of George Eliot

Compiled & edited
by
ODELIA FLORIS

Copyright © Odelia Floris 2018

Earnest Acorn Books
Grow your reading pleasure

Also by Odelia Floris

Nonfiction:
Inspiration & Wisdom from the Pen of Ralph Waldo Emerson: Over 600 Quotes

Adult fiction:
The Heart of Darkness (The Chaucy Shire Medieval Mysteries Book 1)

Beguile Me Not

In Want of a Wife

Rusalka: A Supernatural Czech Fairy tale

Children's fiction:
The Little Demon Who Couldn't

www.odeliafloris.com

Contents

Life and Living................................1

Love and Friendship.......................13

Manners and Speech......................20

People and Character....................25

Wealth and Charity.........................35

Morality and Virtue........................37

Work and Vocation........................44

Knowledge and Truth....................46

The Life of Feeling.........................51

Thoughts..59

Doing..61

God, Religion and Belief...............64

Art and Literature..........................67

Nature and Beauty.........................70

Greatness and Heroism.................75

Life and Living

"What do we live for, if it is not to make life less difficult for each other?"

"It will never rain roses: when we want to have more roses, we must plant more roses."

"It seems to me we can never give up longing and wishing while we are still alive. There are certain things we feel to be beautiful and good, and we must hunger for them."

"A man falling into dark waters seeks a momentary footing even on sliding stones."

"If we had a keen vision and feeling of all ordinary human life, it would be like hearing the grass grow and the squirrel's heart beat, and we should die of that roar which lies on the other side of silence."

"What destroys us most effectively is not a malign fate but our own capacity for self-deception and for degrading our own best self."

"The promise was void, like so many other sweet, illusory promises of our childhood; void as promises made in Eden before the seasons were divided, and when the starry blossoms grew side by side with the ripening peach,—impossible to be fulfilled when the golden gates had been passed."

"If youth is the season of hope, it is often so only in the sense that our elders are hopeful about us; for no age is so apt as youth to think its emotions, partings, and resolves are the last of their kind. Each crisis seems final, simply because it is new."

"It is an uneasy lot at best, to be what we call highly taught and yet not to enjoy: to be present at this great spectacle of life and never to be liberated from a small hungry shivering self – never to be fully possessed by the glory we behold, never to have our consciousness rapturously transformed into the vividness of a thought, the ardor of a passion, the energy of an action, but always to be scholarly and uninspired, ambitious and timid, scrupulous and dim-sighted."

"Starting a long way off the true point by loops and zigags, we now and then arrive just where we ought to be."

"Those bitter sorrows of childhood! – when sorrow is all new and strange, when hope has not yet got wings to fly beyond the days and weeks, and the space from summer to summer seems measureless."

"Every limit is a beginning as well as an ending."

"The progress of the world can certainly never come at all save by the modified action of the individual beings who compose the world."

"Certainly the determining acts of her life were not ideally beautiful. They were the mixed result of young and novel impulse struggling amidst the conditions of an imperfect social state, in which great feelings will often take the aspect of error, and great faith the aspect of illusion."

"The golden moments in the stream of life rush past us and we see nothing but sand; the angels come to visit us, and we only know them when they are gone."

"I would not creep along the coast but steer out in mid-sea, by guidance of the stars."

"She thought it was part of the hardship of her life that there was laid upon her the burthen of larger wants than others seemed to feel – that she had to endure this wide hopeless yearning for that something, whatever it was, that was greatest and best on this earth."

"We all remember epochs in our experience when some dear expectation dies, or some new motive is born."

"When death, the great Reconciler, has come, it is never our tenderness that we repent of, but our severity."

"Only those who know the supremacy of the intellectual life – the life which has a seed of ennobling thought and purpose within – can understand the grief of one who falls from that serene activity into the absorbing soul-wasting struggle with worldly annoyances."

"Destiny stands by sarcastic with our dramatis personae folded in her hand."

"The most solid comfort one can fall back upon is the thought that the business of one's life is to help in some small way to reduce the sum of ignorance, degradation and misery on the face of this beautiful earth."

"If a man goes a little too far along a new road, it is usually himself that he harms more than any one else."

"There is no hopelessness so sad as that of early youth, when the soul is made up of wants, and has no long memories, no super-added life in the life of others; though we who look on think lightly of such premature despair, as if our vision of the future lightened the blind sufferer's present."

"In old days there were angels who came and took men by the hand and led them away from the city of destruction. We see no white-winged angels now. But yet men are led away from threatening destruction: a hand is put into theirs, which leads them forth gently towards a calm and bright land, so that they look no more backward; and the hand may be a little child's."

"They had entered the thorny wilderness, and the golden gates of their childhood had for ever closed behind them."

"In bed our yesterdays are too oppressive: if a man can only get up, though it be but to whistle or to smoke, he has a present which offers some resistance to the past – sensations which assert themselves against tyrannous memories."

"The sense of security more frequently springs from habit than from conviction, and for this reason it often subsists after such a change in the conditions as might have been expected to suggest alarm. The lapse of time during which a given event has not happened, is, in this logic of habit, constantly alleged as a reason why the event should never happen, even when the lapse of time is precisely the added condition which makes the event imminent."

"What should we all do without the calendar, when we want to put off a disagreeable duty? The admirable arrangements of the solar system, by which our time is measured, always supply us with a term before which it is hardly worthwhile to set about anything we are disinclined to."

"But any one watching keenly the stealthy convergence of human lots, sees a slow preparation of effects from one life on another, which tells like a calculated irony on the indifference or the frozen stare with which we look at our unintroduced neighbor."

"In the checkered area of human experience the seasons are all mingled as in the golden age: fruit and blossom hang together; in the same moment the sickle is reaping and the seed is sprinkled; one tends the green cluster and another treads the winepress. Nay, in each of our lives harvest and spring-time are continually one, until himself gathers us and sows us anew in his invisible fields."

"It is in these acts called trivialities that the seeds of joy are forever wasted until men and women look round with haggard faces at the devastation their own waste has made and say the earth bears no harvest of sweetness - calling their denial knowledge."

"I call it improper pride to let fool's notions hinder you from doing a good action. There's no sort of work," said Caleb, with fervor, putting out his hand and moving it up and down to mark his emphasis, "that could ever be done well, if you minded what fools say. You must have it inside you that your plan is right, and that plan you must follow."

"The important work of moving the world forward does not wait to be done by perfect men."

"The limits of variation are really much wider than any one would imagine from the sameness of women's coiffure and the favourite love-stories in prose and verse. Here and there a cygnet is reared uneasily among the ducklings in the brown pond, and never finds the living stream in fellowship with its own oary-footed kind."

"We are on a perilous margin when we begin to look passively at our future selves, and see our own figures led with dull consent into insipid misdoing and shabby achievement."

"Those who have been indulged by fortune and have always thought of calamity as what happens to others, feel a blinding credulous rage at the reversal of their lot and half believe that their wild cries will alter the course of the storm."

"A man conscious of enthusiasm for worthy aims is sustained under petty hostilities by the memory of great workers who had to fight their way not without wounds, and who hover in his mind as patron saints, invisibly helping."

"But with regard to critical occasions, it often happens that all moments seem comfortably remote until the last."

"The only failure a man ought to fear is failure of cleaving to the purpose he sees to be best."

"We know what a masquerade all development is, and what effective shapes may be disguised in helpless embryos.—In fact, the world is full of hopeful analogies and handsome dubious eggs called possibilities."

"When the commonplace 'We must all die' transforms itself suddenly into the acute consciousness 'I must die – and soon,' then death grapples us, and his fingers are cruel; afterwards, he may come to fold us in his arms as our mother did, and our last moment of dim earthly discerning may be like the first."

"Obligation may be stretched till it is no better than a brand of slavery stamped on us when we were too young to know its meaning."

"There is no hour that has not its births of gladness and despair, no morning brightness that does not bring new sickness to desolation as well as new forces to genius and love."

"For the fragment of a life, however typical, is not the sample of an even web: promises may not be kept, and an ardent outset may be followed by declension; latent powers may find their long-awaited opportunity; a past error may urge a grand retrieval."

"It might well happen to most of us dainty people that we were in the thick of the battle of Armageddon without being aware of anything more than the annoyance of a little explosive smoke and struggling on the ground immediately about us."

"It is an old story, that men sell themselves to the tempter, and sign a bond with their blood, because it is only to take effect at a distant day; then rush on to snatch the cup their souls thirst after with an impulse not the less savage because there is a dark shadow beside them forevermore. There is no short cut, no patent tram-road to wisdom: after all the centuries of invention, the soul's path lies through the thorny wilderness which must be still trodden in solitude, with bleeding feet, with sobs for help, as it was trodden by them of old time."

Love, Marriage and Friendship

"I like not only to be loved, but also to be told that I am loved. I am not sure that you are of the same mind. But the realm of silence is large enough beyond the grave. This is the world of light and speech, and I shall take leave to tell you that you are very dear."

"Only in the agony of parting do we look into the depths of love."

"A friend is one to whom one may pour out the contents of one's heart, chaff and grain together, knowing that gentle hands will take and sift it, keep what is worth keeping, and with a breath of kindness, blow the rest away."

"What greater thing is there for two human souls, than to feel that they are joined for life – to strengthen each other in all labor, to rest on each other in all sorrow, to minister to each other in all pain, to be one with each other in silent unspeakable memories at the moment of the last parting?"

"Blessed is the influence of one true, loving human soul on another."

"For what is love itself, for the one we love best? – an enfolding of immeasurable cares which yet are better than any joys outside our love."

"When a man has seen the woman whom he would have chosen if he had intended to marry speedily, his remaining a bachelor will usually depend on her resolution rather than on his."

"Men outlive their love, but they don't outlive the consequences of their recklessness."

"I should never like scolding any one else so well; and that is a point to be thought of in a husband."

"Explain! Tell a man to explain how he dropped into hell! Explain my preference! I never had a *preference* for her, any more than I have a preference for breathing."

"Marriage is so unlike everything else. There is something even awful in the nearness it brings. Even if we loved someone else better than those we were married to, it would be no use. I mean, marriage drinks up all our power of giving or getting any blessedness in that sort of love. I know it may be very dear, but it murders our marriage, and then the marriage stays with us like a murder, and everything else is gone."

"Love has a way of cheating itself consciously, like a child who plays at solitary hide-and-seek; it is pleased with assurances that it all the while disbelieves."

"Perfect love has a breath of poetry which can exalt the relations of the least-instructed human beings."

"Marriage, which has been the bourne of so many narratives, is still a great beginning, as it was to Adam and Eve, who kept their honey-moon in Eden, but had their first little one among the thorns and thistles of the wilderness. It is still the beginning of the home epic – the gradual conquest or irremediable loss of that complete union which make the advancing years a climax, and age the harvest of sweet memories in common."

"How is it that the poets have said so many fine things about our first love, so few about our later love? Are their first poems their best? Or are not those the best which come from their fuller thought, their larger experience, their deeper-rooted affections?"

"Wear a smile and have friends; wear a scowl and have wrinkles."

"It is a wonderful subduer, this need of love – this hunger of the heart – as peremptory as that other hunger by which Nature forces us to submit to the yoke, and change the face of the world."

"When a tender affection has been storing itself in us through many of our years, the idea that we could accept any exchange for it seems to be a cheapening of our lives."

"We can set a watch over our affections and our constancy as we can over other treasures."

"Society never made the preposterous demand that a man should think as much about his own qualifications for making a charming girl happy as he thinks of hers for making himself happy."

"It is easy to say how we love new friends, and what we think of them, but words can never trace out all the fibers that knit us to the old."

"That's the way with 'em all: it's as if they thought the world 'ud be new-made because they're to be married."

"I suppose it was that in courtship everything is regarded as provisional and preliminary, and the smallest sample of virtue or accomplishment is taken to guarantee delightful stores which the broad leisure of marriage will reveal. But the door-sill of marriage once crossed, expectation is concentrated on the present."

"Mrs. Tulliver, as we have seen, was not without influence over her husband. No woman is; she can always incline him to do either what she wishes, or the reverse."

"'I don't see how a man is to be good for much unless he has some one woman to love him dearly.' – 'I think the goodness should come before he expects that.'"

"A man with an affectionate disposition, who finds a wife to concur with his fundamental idea of life, easily comes to persuade himself that no other woman would have suited him so well, and does a little daily snapping and quarreling without any sense of alienation."

Manners and Speech

"Self-consciousness of the manner is the expensive substitute for simplicity."

"There are answers which, in turning away wrath, only send it to the other end of the room, and to have a discussion coolly waived when you feel that justice is all on your own side is even more exasperating in marriage than in philosophy."

"The wit of a family is usually best received among strangers."

"It is offensive to tell a lady when she is expressing her amazement at your skill, that she is altogether mistaken and rather foolish in her amazement."

"I suppose one reason why we are seldom able to comfort our neighbours with our words is that our good will gets adulterated, in spite of ourselves, before it can pass our lips. We can send black puddings and potatoes without giving them a flavour of our own egoism; but language is a stream that is almost sure to smack of a mingled soil."

"Speech is but broken light upon the depth of the unspoken."

"'All choice of words is slang. It marks a class." - 'There is correct English: that is not slang.' - 'I beg your pardon: correct English is the slang of prigs who write history and essays. And the strongest slang of all is the slang of poets.'"

"It was one of those dangerous moments when speech is at once sincere and deceptive, when feeling, rising high above its average depth, leaves flood-marks which are never reached again."

"Even when she was speaking, her soul was in prayer reposing on an unseen support."

"Blessed is the man who, having nothing to say, abstains from giving us wordy evidence of the fact."

"Few things hold the perception more thoroughly captive than anxiety about what we have got to say."

"Of course people need not be always talking well. Only one tells the quality of their minds when they try to talk well."

People and Character

"And, of course men know best about everything, except what women know better."

"Adventure is not outside man; it is within."

"We mortals, men and women, devour many a disappointment between breakfast and dinner-time; keep back the tears and look a little pale about the lips, and in answer to inquiries say, 'Oh, nothing!' Pride helps; and pride is not a bad thing when it only urges us to hide our hurts – not to hurt others."

"Selfish – a judgment readily passed by those who have never tested their own power of sacrifice."

"One can begin so many things with a new person! – even begin to be a better man."

"And certainly, the mistakes that we male and female mortals make when we have our own way might fairly raise some wonder that we are so fond of it."

"People are almost always better than their neighbors think they are."

"The presence of a noble nature, generous in its wishes, ardent in its charity, changes the lights for us: we begin to see things again in their larger, quieter masses, and to believe that we too can be seen and judged in the wholeness of our character."

"The troublesome ones in a family are usually either the wits or the idiots."

"Character is not cut in marble - it is not something solid and unalterable. It is something living and changing, and may become diseased as our bodies do."

"Sane people did what their neighbors did, so that if any lunatics were at large, one might know and avoid them."

"Blameless people are always the most exasperating."

"A prig is a fellow who is always making you a present of his opinions."

"Who can all at once describe a human being? Even when he is presented to us we only begin that knowledge of his appearance which must be completed by innumerable impressions under differing circumstances."

"She hates everything that is not what she longs for."

"We must learn to accommodate ourselves to the discovery that some of those cunningly-fashioned instruments called human souls have only a very limited range of music, and will not vibrate in the least under a touch that fills others with tremulous rapture or quivering agony."

"We have all a chance of meeting with some pity, some tenderness, some charity, when we are dead: it is the living only who cannot be forgiven – the living only from whom men's indulgence and reverence are held off, like the rain by the hard east wind."

"How can a man's candour be seen in all its lustre unless he has a few failings to talk of?"

"Those who trust us educate us."

"A medical man likes to make psychological observations, and sometimes in the pursuit of such studies is too easily tempted into momentous prophecy which life and death easily set at nought."

"I think there are stores laid up in our human nature that our understandings can make no complete inventory of."

"But how little we know what would make paradise for our neighbors. We judge from our own desires, and our neighbors themselves are not always open enough even to throw out a hint of theirs."

"These fellow-mortals, every one, must be accepted as they are: you can neither straighten their noses, nor brighten their wit, nor rectify their dispositions; and it is these people – amongst whom your life is passed – that it is needful you should tolerate, pity, and love: it is these more or less ugly, stupid, inconsistent people, whose movements of goodness you should be able to admire – for whom you should cherish all possible hopes, all possible patience."

"It's easy finding reasons why other folks should be patient."

"For there is no creature whose inward being is so strong that it is not greatly determined by what lies outside it."

"Family likeness has often a deep sadness in it. Nature, that great tragic dramatist, knits us together by bone and muscle, and divides us by the subtler web of our brains; blends yearning and repulsion; and ties us by our heart-strings to the beings that jar us at every movement."

"Souls have complexions too: what will suit one will not suit another."

"We are all of us denying or fulfilling prayers - and men in their careless deeds walk amidst invisible outstretched arms and pleadings made in vain."

"When we are treated well, we naturally begin to think that we are not altogether unmeritorious, and that it is only just we should treat ourselves well, and not mar our own good fortune."

"It is curious what patches of hardness and tenderness lie side by side in men's dispositions."

"Let even an affectionate Goliath get himself tied to a small tender thing, dreading to hurt it by pulling, and dreading still more to snap the cord, and which of the two, pray, will be master?"

"Here and there is born a Saint Theresa, foundress of nothing, whose loving heart-beats and sobs after an unattained goodness tremble off and are dispersed among hindrances, instead of centering in some long-recognizable deed."

"She had forgotten his faults as we forget the sorrows of our departed childhood."

"Our consiousness rarely registers the beginning of a growth within us anymore than without us: there have been many circulations of the sap before we detect the smallest sign of the bud."

"The happiest women, like the happiest nations, have no history."

"Men, like planets, have both a visible and an invisible history. The astronomer threads the darkness with strict deduction, accounting so for every visible arc in the wanderer's orbit; and the narrator of human actions, if he did his work with the same completeness, would have to thread the hidden pathways of feeling and thought which lead up to every moment of action, and to those moments of intense suffering which take the quality of action – like the cry of Prometheus, whose chained anguish seems a greater energy than the sea and sky he invokes and the deity he defies."

"Dorothea, he said to himself, was for ever enthroned in his soul: no other woman could sit higher than her footstool."

"One's self-satisfaction is an untaxed kind of property which it is very unpleasant to find deprecated."

"The kindness fell on him as sunshine falls on the wretched – he had no heart to taste it, and felt that it was very far off him."

"I should like to know what is the proper function of women, if it is not to make reasons for husbands to stay at home, and still stronger reasons for bachelors to go out."

"His soul was sensitive without being enthusiastic: it was too languid to thrill out of self-consciousness into passionate delight; it went on fluttering in the swampy ground where it was hatched, thinking of its wings and never flying."

"The existence of insignificant people has very important consequences in the world. It can be shown to affect the price of bread and the rate of wages, to call forth many evil tempers from the selfish and many heroisms from the sympathetic, and, in other ways, to play no small part in the tragedy of life."

"Don't you think men overrate the necessity for humoring everybody's nonsense, till they get despised by the very fools they humor?"

"It is our habit to say that while the lower nature can never understand the higher, the higher nature commands a complete view of the lower. But I think the higher nature has to learn this comprehension, as we learn the art of vision, by a good deal of hard experience, often with bruises and gashes incurred in taking things up by the wrong end, and fancying our space wider than it is."

"In so complex a thing as human nature, we must consider, it is hard to find rules without exception."

"People were so ridiculous with their illusions, carrying their fool's caps unawares, thinking their own lies opaque while everybody else's were transparent, making themselves exceptions to everything, as if when all the world looked yellow under a lamp they alone were rosy."

"I've never any pity for conceited people, because I think they carry their comfort about with them."

"A man carries within him the germ of his most exceptional action; and if we wise people make eminent fools of ourselves on any particular occasion, we must endure the legitimate conclusion that we carry a few grains of folly to our ounce of wisdom."

"A kind Providence furnishes the limpest personality with a little gum or starch in the form of tradition."

"There are characters which are continually creating collisions and nodes for themselves in dramas which nobody is prepared to act with them. Their susceptibilities will clash against objects that remain innocently quiet."

"To most mortals there is a stupidity which is unendurable and a stupidity which is altogether acceptable — else, indeed, what would become of social bonds?"

"I'm not denyin' the women are foolish; God Almighty made 'em to match the men."

"That was the way with Casaubon's hard intellectual labours. Their most characteristic result was not the 'Key to all Mythologies', but a morbid consciousness that others did not give him the place which he had not demonstrably merited – a perpetual suspicious conjecture that the views entertained of him were not to his advantage – a melancholy absence of passion in his efforts at achievement, and a passionate resistance to the confession that he had achieved nothing."

Wealth and Charity

"One must be poor to know the luxury of giving."

"It's rather a strong check to one's self-complacency to find how much of one's right doing depends on not being in want of money."

"We may handle even extreme opinions with impunity while our furniture, our dinner giving, and preference for armorial bearings in our own case link us indissolubly with the established order."

"I've always felt that your belongings have never been on a level with you."

"But we all know the wag's definition of a philanthropist: a man whose charity increases directly as the square of the distance."

"I fear that in this thing many rich people deceive themselves. They go on accumulating the means but never using them; making bricks, but never building."

Morality and Virtue

"It is surely better to pardon too much, than to condemn too much."

"But the effect of her being on those around her was incalculably diffusive: for the growing good of the world is partly dependent on unhistoric acts; and that things are not so ill with you and me as they might have been, is half owing to the number who lived faithfully a hidden life, and rest in unvisited tombs."

"The terror of being judged sharpens the memory: it sends an inevitable glare over that long-unvisited past which has been habitually recalled only in general phrases. Even without memory, the life is bound into one by a zone of dependence in growth and decay; but intense memory forces a man to own his blameworthy past. With memory set smarting like a reopened wound, a man's past is not simply a dead history, an outworn preparation of the present: it is not a repented error shaken loose from the life: it is a still quivering part of himself, bringing shudders and bitter flavors and the tinglings of a merited shame.

"Let my body dwell in poverty, and my hands be as the hands of the toiler; but let my soul be as a temple of remembrance where the treasures of knowledge enter and the inner sanctuary is hope."

"Pride only helps us to be generous; it never makes us so, any more than vanity makes us witty."

"No evil dooms us hopelessly except the evil we love, and desire to continue in, and make no effort to escape from."

"My own experience and development deepen every day my conviction that our moral progress may be measured by the degree in which we sympathize with individual suffering and individual joy."

"Cruelty, like every other vice, requires no motive outside of itself; it only requires opportunity."

"Among all forms of mistake, prophecy is the most gratuitous."

"We cannot speak a loyal word and be meanly silent, we cannot kill and not kill in the same moment; but a moment is room wide enough for the loyal and mean desire, for the outlash of a murderous thought and the sharp backward stroke of repetance."

"There is no general doctrine which is not capable of eating out our morality if unchecked by the deep-seated habit of direct fellow-feeling with individual fellow-men."

"Mortals are easily tempted to pinch the life out of their neighbor's buzzing glory, and think that such killing is no murder."

"The yoke a man creates for himself by wrong-doing will breed hate in the kindliest nature."

"By desiring what is perfectly good, even when we don't quite know what it is and cannot do what we would, we are part of the divine power against evil - widening the skirts of light and making the struggle with darkness narrower."

"We are all of us born in moral stupidity, taking the world as an udder to feed our supreme selves"

"Who with repentance is not satisfied, is not of heaven, nor earth."

"So deeply inherent is it in this life of ours that men have to suffer for each other's sins, so inevitably diffusive is human suffering, that even justice makes its victims, and we can conceive no retribution that does not spread beyond its mark in pulsations of unmerited pain."

"Duty has a trick of behaving unexpectedly – something like a heavy friend whom we have amiably asked to visit us, and who breaks his leg within our gates."

"The reward of one duty is the power to fulfill another."

"Our good depends on the quality and breadth of our emotions."

"Our guides, we pretend, must be sinless: as if those were not often the best teachers who only yesterday got corrected for their mistakes."

"Conscience is harder than our enemies, knows more, accuses with more nicety."

"But I wasn't worth doing wrong for – nothing is in this world. Nothing is so good as it seems beforehand."

"I think we have no right to come forward and urge wider changes for good, until we have tried to alter the evils which lie under our own hands."

"The prevarication and white lies which a mind that keeps itself ambitiously pure is as uneasy under as a great artist under the false touches that no eye detects but his own, are worn as lightly as mere trimming when once the actions have become a lie."

"But he had something else to curse – his own viscious folly, which now seemed as mad and unaccountable to him as almost all our follies and vices do when their promptings have long passed away."

"Soul of man, when it gets fairly rotten, will bear you all sorts of poisonous toad-stools, and no eye can see whence came the seed thereof."

Work and Vocation

"You must love your work, and not be always looking over the edge of it, wanting your play to begin. And the other is, you must not be ashamed of your work, and think it would be more honorable to you to be doing something else. You must have a pride in your own work and in learning to do it well, and not be always saying, There's this and there's that – if I had this or that to do, I might make something of it."

"After all, people may really have in them some vocation which is not quite plain to themselves, may they not? They may seem idle and weak because they are growing. We should be very patient with each other, I think."

"For in the multitude of middle-aged men who go about their vocations in a daily course determined for them much in the same way as the tie of their cravats, there is always a good number who once meant to shape their own deeds and alter the world a little. The story of their coming to be shapen after the average and fit to be packed by the gross, is hardly ever told even in their consciousness; for perhaps their ardour in generous unpaid toil cooled as imperceptibly as the ardour of other youthful loves, till one day their earlier self walked like a ghost in its old home and made the new furniture ghastly."

"If I got places, sir, it was because I made myself fit for 'em. If you want to slip into a round hole, you must first make a ball of yourself; that's where it is."

"Every man's work, pursued steadily, tends to become an end in itself, and so to bridge over the loveless chasms of his life."

Knowledge and Truth

"It is a narrow mind which cannot look at a subject from various points of view."

"It is a common sentence that knowledge is power; but who hath duly considered or set forth the power of ignorance? Knowledge slowly builds up what ignorance in an hour pulls down."

"If you deliver an opinion at all, it is mere stupidity not to do it with an air of conviction and well-founded knowledge. You make it your own in uttering it, and naturally get fond of it."

"More helpful than all wisdom is one draught of simple human pity that will not forsake us."

"It is very hard to say the exact truth, even about your own immediate feelings – much harder than to say something fine about them which is not the exact truth."

"The memory has as many moods as the temper, and shifts its scenery like a diorama."

"Will not a tiny speck very close to our vision blot out the glory of the world, and leave only a margin by which we see the blot? I know no speck so troublesome as self."

"Upon my word, I think the truth is the hardest missile one can be pelted with."

"The dull mind, once arriving at an inference that flatters the desire, is rarely able to retain the impression that the notion from which the inference started was purely problematic."

"After all, the true seeing is within."

"All people of broad, strong sense have an instinctive repugnance to the men of maxims; because such people early discern that the mysterious complexity of our life is not to be embraced by maxims, and that to lace ourselves up in formulas of that sort is to repress all the divine promptings and inspirations that spring from growing insight and sympathy."

"Probabilities - the surest screen a wise man can place between himself and the truth."

"All meanings, we know, depend on the key of interpretation."

"Our sweet illusions are half of them conscious illusions, like effects of colour that we know to be made up of tinsel, broken glass and rags."

"If there is an angel who records the sorrows of men as well as their sins, he knows how many and deep are the sorrows that spring from false ideas for which no man is culpable."

"No retrospect will take us to the true beginning"

"There is hardly any contact more depressing to a young ardent creature than that of a mind in which years full of knowledge seem to have issued in a blank absence of interest or sympathy."

"What we call the 'just possible' is sometimes true and the thing we find it easier to believe is grossly false."

"For getting a fine flourishing growth of stupidity there is nothing like pouring out on a mind a good amount of subjects in which it feels no interest."

"Scepticism, as we know, can never be thoroughly applied, else life would come to a standstill"

"We begin by knowing little and believing much, and we sometimes end by inverting the quantities."

"As it is, the quickest of us walk about well wadded with stupidity."

"To glory in a prophetic vision of knowledge covering the earth, is an easier exercise of believing imagination than to see its beginning in newspaper placards, staring at you from the bridge beyond the corn-fields."

"We are all humiliated by the sudden discovery of a fact which has existed very comfortably and perhaps been staring at us in private while we have been making up our world entirely without it."

"Truth has rough flavours if we bite it through."

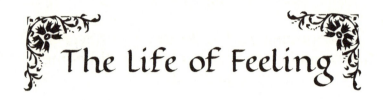

The Life of Feeling

"What loneliness is more lonely than distrust?"

"What we call our despair is often only the painful eagerness of unfed hope."

"There is no despair so absolute as that which comes from the first moments of our first great sorrow when we have not yet known what it is to have suffered and healed, to have despaired and recovered hope."

"Jealousy is never satisfied with anything short of an omniscience that would detect the subtlest fold of the heart."

"Anxiety is good for nothing if we can't turn it into a defense."

"There is something sustaining in the very agitation that accompanies the first shocks of trouble, just as an acute pain is often a stimulus, and produces an excitement which is transient strength."

"There is a great deal of unmapped country within us which would have to be taken into account in an explanation of our gusts and storms."

"Anger and jealousy can no more bear to lose sight of their objects than love."

"There is a sort of jealousy which needs very little fire: it is hardly a passion, but a blight bred in the cloudy, damp despondency of uneasy egoism."

"Thank God; human feeling is like the mighty rivers that bless the earth: it does not wait for beauty - it flows with resistless force and brings beauty with it."

"There is much pain that is quite noiseless; and vibrations that make human agonies are often a mere whisper in the roar of hurrying existence. There are glances of hatred that stab and raise no cry of murder; robberies that leave man or woman forever beggared of peace and joy, yet kept secret by the sufferer – committed to no sound except that of low moans in the night, seen in no writing except that made on the face by the slow months of suppressed anguish and early morning tears. Many an inherited sorrow that has marred a life has been breathed into no human ear."

"It is seldom that the miserable can help regarding their misery as a wrong inflicted by those who are less miserable"

"We are all of us imaginative in some form or other, for images are the brood of desire."

"Doubtless a great anguish may do the work of years, and we may come out from that baptism of fire with a soul full of new awe and new pity."

"To have in general but little feeling, seems to be the only security against feeling too much on any particular occasion."

"Strange, that some of us, with quick alternative vision, see beyond our infatuations, and even while we rave on the heights, behold the wide plain where our persistent self pauses and awaits us."

"There are conditions under which the most majestic person is obliged to sneeze, and our emotions are liable to be acted on in the same incongruous manner."

"Passion is of the nature of seed, and finds nourishment within, tending to a predominance which determines all currents towards itself, and makes the whole life its tributary."

"A man never lies with more delicious languor under the influence of a passion than when he has persuaded himself that he shall subdue it to-morrow."

"Joy and peace are not resignation: resignation is the willing endurance of a pain that is not allayed – that you don't expect to be allayed. Stupefaction is not resignation: and it is stupefaction to remain in ignorance – to shut up all the avenues by which the life of your fellow-men might become known to you. I am not resigned: I am not sure that life is long enough to learn that lesson. You are not resigned: you are only trying to stupefy yourself."

"Take your sensibility and use it as a vision"

"There are few prophets in the world; few sublimely beautiful women; few heroes. I can't afford to give all my love and reverence to such rarities: I want a great deal of those feelings for my every-day fellow-men, especially for the few in the foreground of the great multitude, whose faces I know, whose hands I touch, for whom I have to make way with kindly courtesy."

"There may be coarse hypocrites, who consciously affect beliefs and emotions for the sake of gulling the world, but Bulstrode was not one of them. He was simply a man whose desires had been stronger than his theoretic beliefs, and who had gradually explained the gratification of his desires into satisfactory agreement with those beliefs. If this be hypocrisy, it is a process which shows itself occasionally in us all."

"The secret of our emotions never lies in the bare object, but in its subtle relations to our own past."

"His experience was of that pitiable kind which shrinks from pity, and fears most of all that is should be known: it was that proud narrow sensitiveness which has not mass enough to spare for transformation into sympathy, and quivers threadlike in small currents of self-preoccupation or at best of an egoistic scrupulosity. "

"In our instinctive rebellion against pain, we are children again, and demand an active will to wreak our vengeance on."

"It would be a poor result of all our anguish and our wrestling if we won nothing but our old selves at the end of it – if we could return to the same blind loves, the same self-confident blame, the same light thoughts of human suffering, the same frivolous gossip over blighted human lives, the same feeble sense of the Unknown towards which we have sent forth irrepressible cries in our loneliness. Let us rather be thankful that our sorrow lives in us as an indestructable force, only changing its form, as forces do, and passing from pain into sympathy – the one poor word which includes all our best insight and our best love."

"It is the favourite stratagem of our passions to sham a retreat, and to turn sharp round upon us at the moment we have made up our minds that the day is our own."

"Men and women make sad mistakes about their own symptoms, taking their vague, uneasy longings sometimes for genius, sometimes for religion, and oftener still for a mighty love."

"Our passions do not live apart in locked chambers, but, dressed in their small wardrobe of notions, bring their provisions to a common table and mess together, feeding out of the common store according to their appetite."

"It seems right to me sometimes that we should follow our strongest feeling; but then, such feelings continually come across the ties that our former life has made for us – the ties that have made others dependent on us – and would cut them in two."

Thoughts

"For we all of us, grave or light, get our thoughts entangled in metaphors, and act fatally on the strength of them."

"It is very difficult to be learned; it seems as if people were worn out on the way to great thoughts, and can never enjoy them because they are too tired."

"No chemical process shows a more wonderful activity than the transforming influence of the thoughts we imagine to be going on in another."

"Uncomfortable thoughts must be got rid of by good intentions for the future."

"Who can know how much of his most inward life is made up of the thoughts he believes other men to have about him, until that fabric of opinion is threatened with ruin?"

"When uncultured minds, confined to a narrow range of personal experience, are under the pressure of continued misfortune, their inward life is apt to become a perpetually repeated round of sad and bitter thoughts: the same words, the same scenes are revolved over and over again, the same mood accompanies them – the end of the year finds them as much what they were at the beginning as if they were machines set to a recurrent series of movements."

"For the egoism which enters into our theories does not affect their sincerity; rather, the more our egoism is satisfied, the more robust is our belief."

"Bodily haste and exertion usually leave our thoughts very much at the mercy of our feelings and imagination."

Doing

"I am not imposed upon by fine words; I can see what actions mean."

"Pity that consequences are determined not by excuses but by actions!"

"If we only look far enough off for the consequence of our actions, we can always find some point in the combination of results by which those actions can be justified: by adopting the point of view of a Providence who arranges results, or of a philosopher who traces them, we shall find it possible to obtain perfect complacency in choosing to do what is most agreeable to us in the present moment."

"It is one thing to like defiance, and another thing to like its consequences."

"I think any hardship is better than pretending to do what one is paid for, and never really doing it."

"Our sense of duty must often wait for some work which shall take the place of dilettanteism and make us feel that the quality of our action is not a matter of indifference."

"Our deeds still travel with us from afar, and what we have been makes us what we are."

"But indefinite visions of ambition are weak against the ease of doing what is habitual or beguilingly agreeable; and we all know the difficulty of carrying out a resolve when we secretly long that it may turn out to be unnecessary. In such states of mind the most incredulous person has a private leaning towards miracle: impossible to conceive how our wish could be fulfilled, still – very wonderful things have happened!"

"Our deeds determine us, as much as we determine our deeds."

"I daresay some would never get their eyes opened if it were not for a violent shock from the consequences of their own actions."

God, Religion and Belief

"I have always been thinking of the different ways in which Christianity is taught, and whenever I find one way that makes it a wider blessing than any other, I cling to that as the truest."

"When God makes His presence felt through us, we are like the burning bush: Moses never took any heed what sort of bush it was - he only saw the brightness of the Lord."

"The most powerful movement of feeling with a liturgy is the prayer which seeks for nothing special, but is a yearning to escape from the limitations of our own weakness and an invocation of all Good to enter and abide with us."

"We are overhasty to speak as if God did not manifest himself by our silent feeling, and make his love felt through ours."

"The religion of personal fear remains nearly at the level of the savage."

"Religious ideas have the fate of melodies, which, once set afloat in the world, are taken up by all sorts of instruments, some of them woefully coarse, feeble, or out of tune, until people are in danger of crying out that the melody itself is detestable."

"Does any one suppose that private prayer is necessarily candid - necessarily goes to the roots of action? Private prayer is inaudible speech, and speech is representative: who can represent himself just as he is, even in his own reflections?"

Art and literature

"It is always fatal to have music or poetry interrupted."

"To be a poet is to have a soul so quick to discern, that no shade of quality escapes it, and so quick to feel, that discernment is but a hand playing with finely-ordered variety on the chords of emotion – a soul in which knowledge passes instantaneously into feeling, and feeling flashes back as a new organ of knowledge."

"There is no feeling, except the extremes of fear and grief, that does not find relief in music."

"No story is the same to us after a lapse of time; or rather we who read it are no longer the same interpreters."

"We learn words by rote, but not their meaning; that must be paid for with our life-blood, and printed in the subtle fibres of our nerves."

"If Art does not enlarge men's sympathies, it does nothing morally."

"The greatest benefit we owe to the artist, whether painter, poet, or novelist, is the extension of our sympathies. Art is the nearest thing to life; it is a mode of amplifying experience and extending our contact with our fellow-men beyond the bounds of our personal lot."

"I have the conviction that excessive literary production is a social offence."

"Some gentlemen have made an amazing figure in literature by general discontent with the universe as a trap of dullness into which their great souls have fallen by mistake."

Nature and Beauty

"There is one order of beauty which seems made to turn heads. It is a beauty like that of kittens, or very small downy ducks making gentle rippling noises with their soft bills, or babies just beginning to toddle."

"We could never have loved the earth so well if we had had no childhood in it."

"Let all plain young ladies be warned against the dangerous encouragement given them by Society to confinde in their want of beauty."

"Is not this a true autumn day? Just the still melancholy that I love – that makes life and nature harmonize. The birds are consulting about their migrations, the trees are putting on the hectic or the pallid hues of decay, and begin to strew the ground, that one's very footsteps may not disturb the repose of earth and air, while they give us a scent that is a perfect anodyne to the restless spirit. Delicious autumn! My very soul is wedded to it, and if I were a bird I would fly about the earth seeking the successive autumns."

"Animals are such agreeable friends - they ask no questions, they pass no criticisms."

"Our caresses, our tender words, our still rapture under the influence of autumn sunsets, or pillared vistas, or calm majestic statues, or Beethoven symphonies, all bring with them the consciousness that they are mere waves and ripples in an unfathomable ocean of love and beauty; our emotion in its keenest moment passes from expression to silence, our love at its highest flood rushes beyond its object, and loses itself in the sense of divine mystery."

"He yearned with a poet's yearning for the wide sky, the far-reaching vista of bridges, the tender and fluctuating lights on the water which seems to breathe with a life that can shiver and mourn, be comforted and rejoice."

Greatness and Heroism

"Genius at first is little more than a great capacity for receiving discipline."

"People glorify all sorts of bravery except the bravery they might show on behalf of their nearest neighbors."

"Any coward can fight a battle when he's sure of winning; but give me the man who has pluck to fight when he's sure of losing. That's my way, sir; and there are many victories worse than a defeat."

"It will always remain true that if we had been greater, circumstance would have been less strong against us."

"We are poor plants buoyed up by the air-vessels of our own conceit: alas for us, if we get a few pinches that empty us of that windy self-subsistence! The very capacity for good would go out of us. For, tell the most impassioned orator, suddenly, that his wig is awry, or his shirt-lap hanging out, and that he is tickling people by the oddity of his person, instead of thrilling them by the energy of his periods, and you would infallibly dry up the spring of his eloquence. That is a deep and wide saying, that no miracle can be wrought without faith – without the worker's faith in himself, as well as the recipient's faith in him. And the greater part of the worker's faith in himself is made up of the faith that others believe in him."

"By a peculiar thermometric adjustment, when a woman's talent is at zero, journalistic approbation is at the boiling pitch; when she attains mediocrity, it is already at no more than summer heat; and if ever she reaches excellence, critical enthusiasm drops to the freezing point."

Note from the Publisher

If you enjoyed this quote collection, you are sure to enjoy its companion volume, *Inspiration & Wisdom from the Pen of Ralph Waldo Emerson*.

Over 600 Quotes

This book presents over 600 quotes for wisdom, inspiration, motivation and living by, each one a gem whose beautiful light will illuminate. Broadly arranged by category, they are carefully chosen and attractively laid out. Ralph Waldo Emerson's insightful, wisdom-filled words are as relevant now as they were when written over 150 years ago. If you are looking for profound yet simple maxims to live by, this book will be an invaluable friend and guide.

The paperback is available on Amazon for just $7.99 USD. You can also download the Kindle edition for only $0.99 or read it with Kindle Unlimited.

And lastly, please take a few minutes to leave a brief review on Amazon. Authors and publishers are always extremely grateful to receive them. Earnest Acorn Books would love to have yours!

Made in the USA
Las Vegas, NV
18 May 2021